I am

by Chris Lensch

This book is dedicated to everyone that works so hard
to make sure that each child feels special.

-Chris

First published by Experience Early Learning Co.
7243 Scotchwood Lane, Grawn, Michigan 49637 USA

ISBN: 978-1-937954-42-0
Visit us at www.ExperienceEarlyLearning.com

I am

by Chris Lensch

I am excited.

I am
sad.

I am curious.

I am sick.

I am brave.

I am shy.

I am
silly.

I am
bored.

I am thoughtful.

I am afraid.

I am
happy.

I am frustrated.

I am proud.

I am worried.

I am angry.

I am
loved.

And that makes all the
different ways I feel okay.

The End